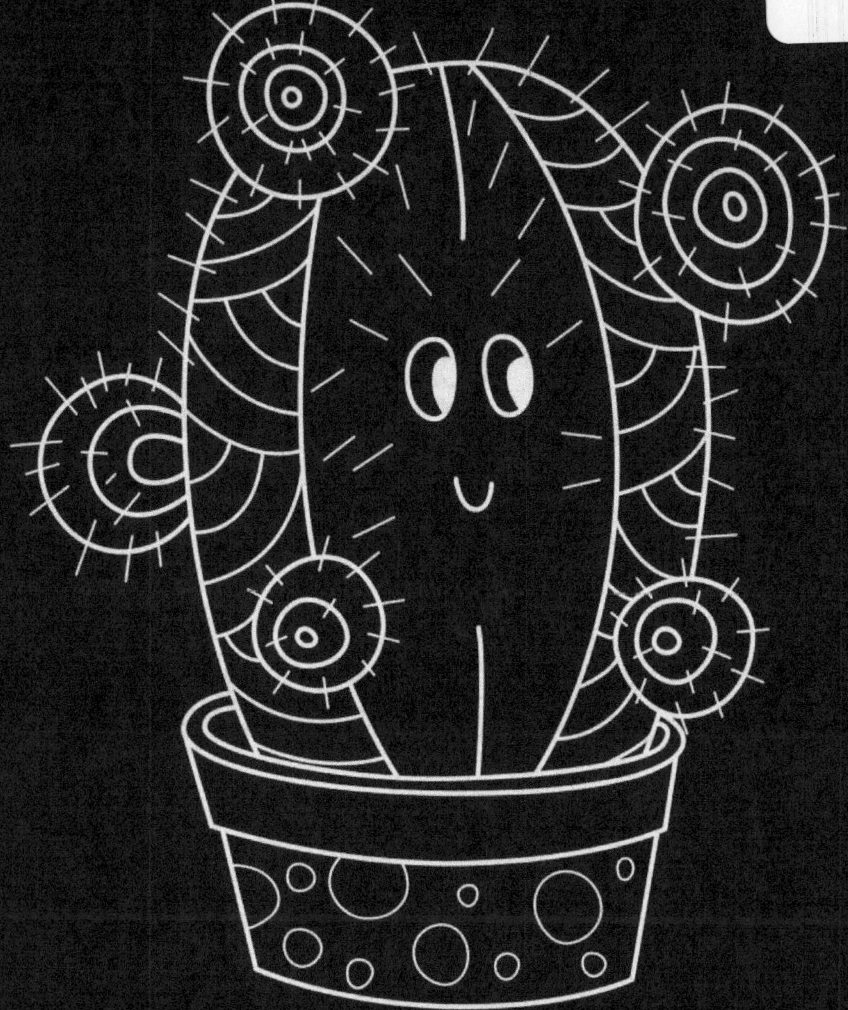

TINY CACTUS PUBLISHING

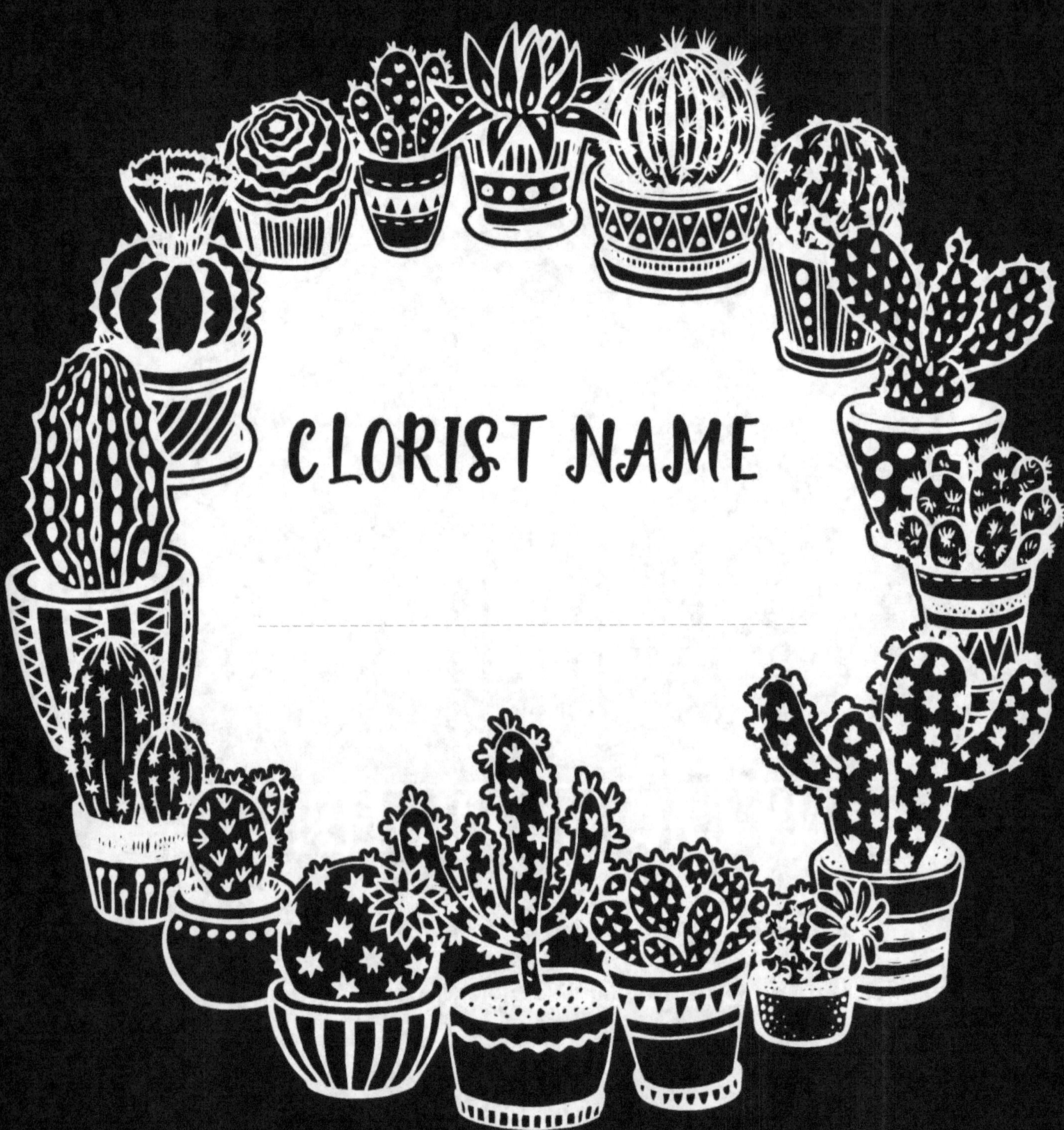

CLORIST NAME

TEST PAGE

PREPARE YOUR COLOR

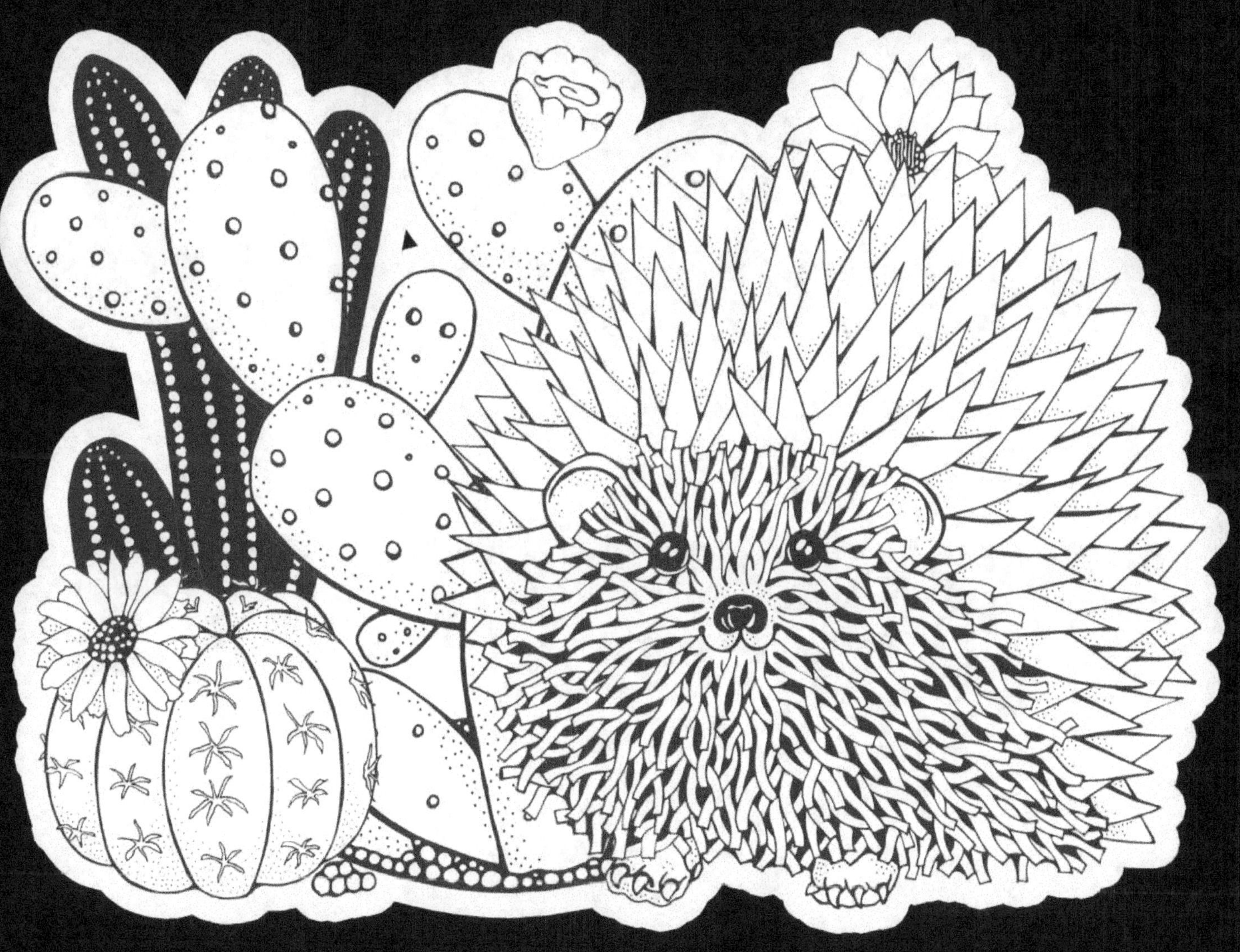

WARM UP !!

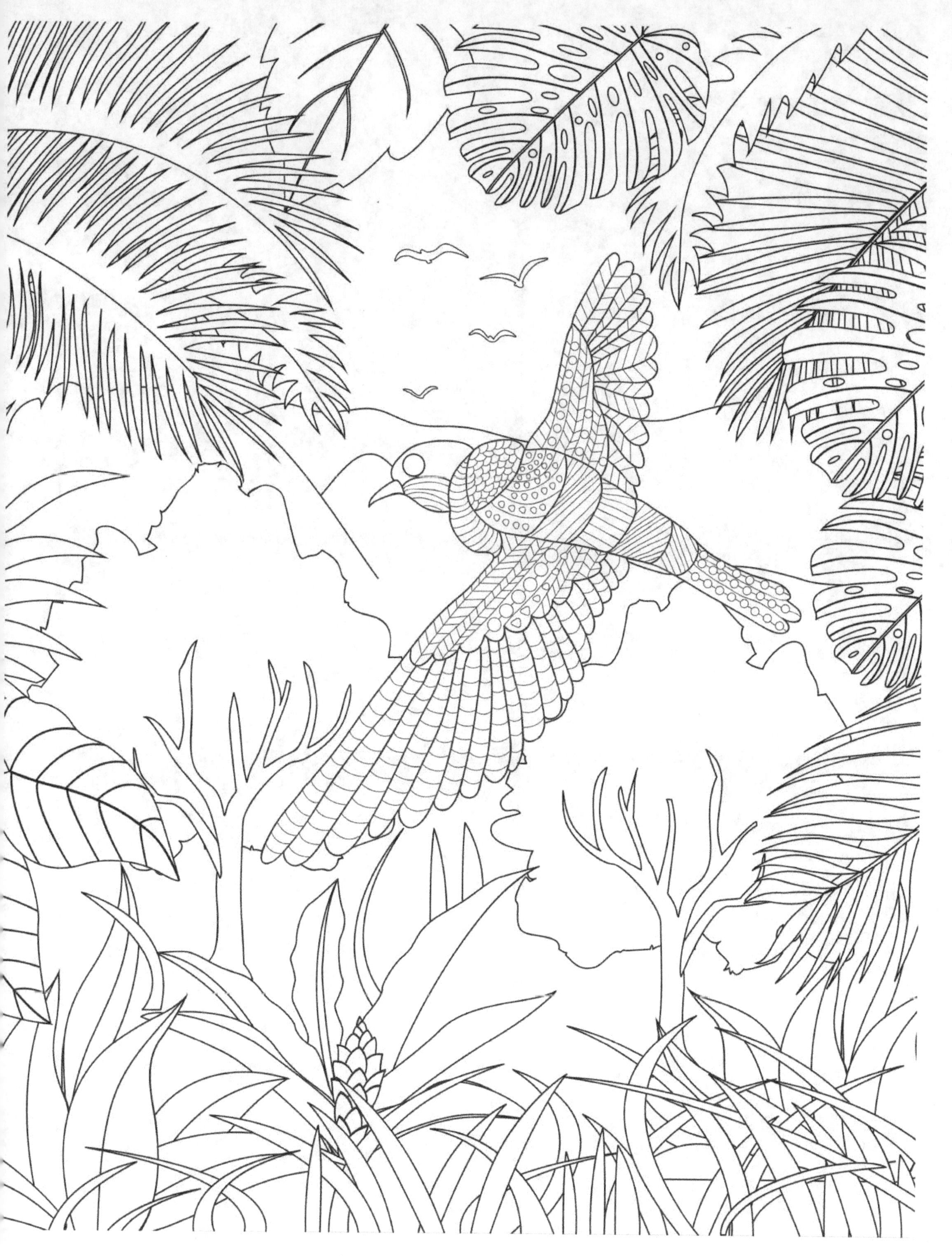

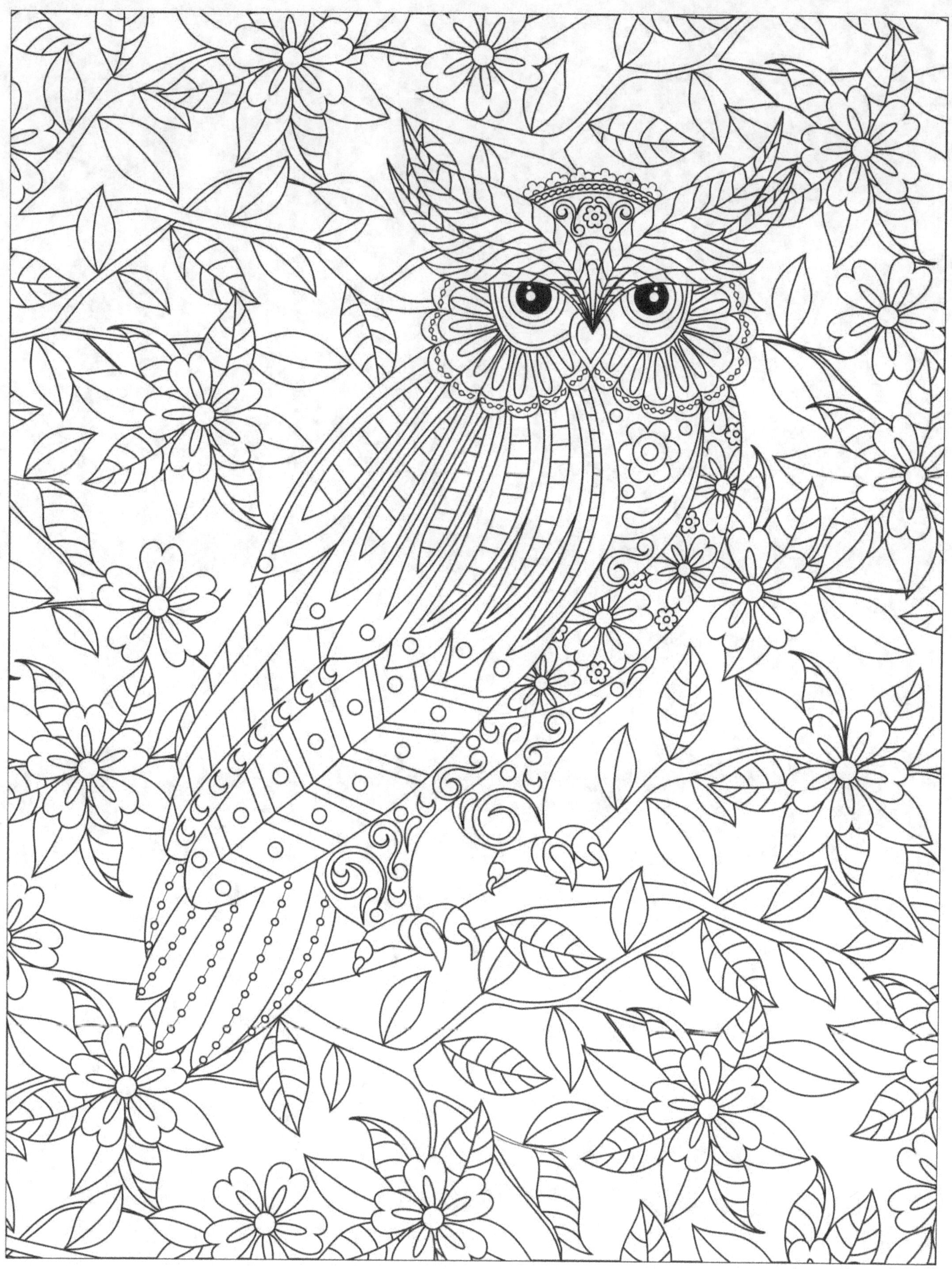

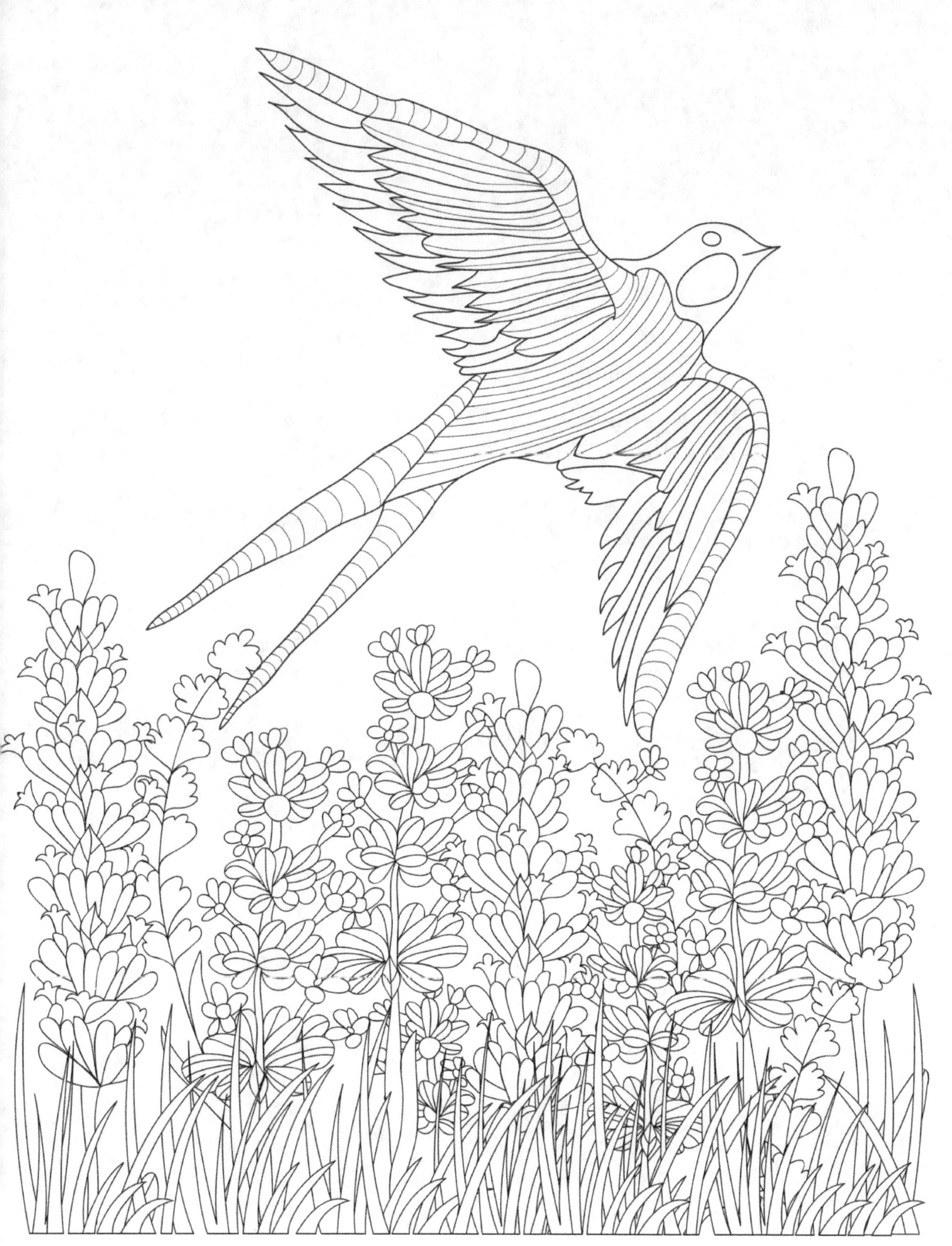

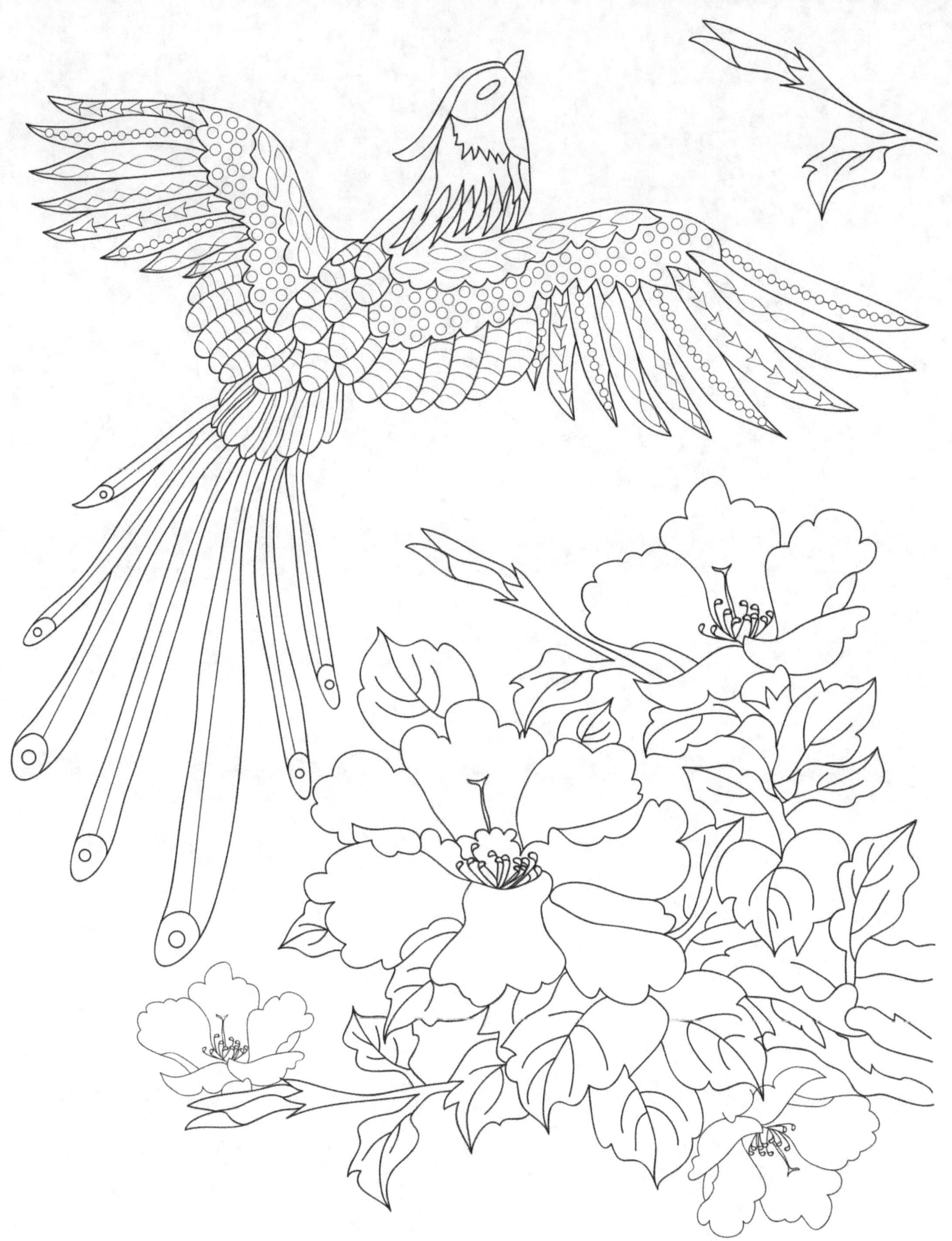

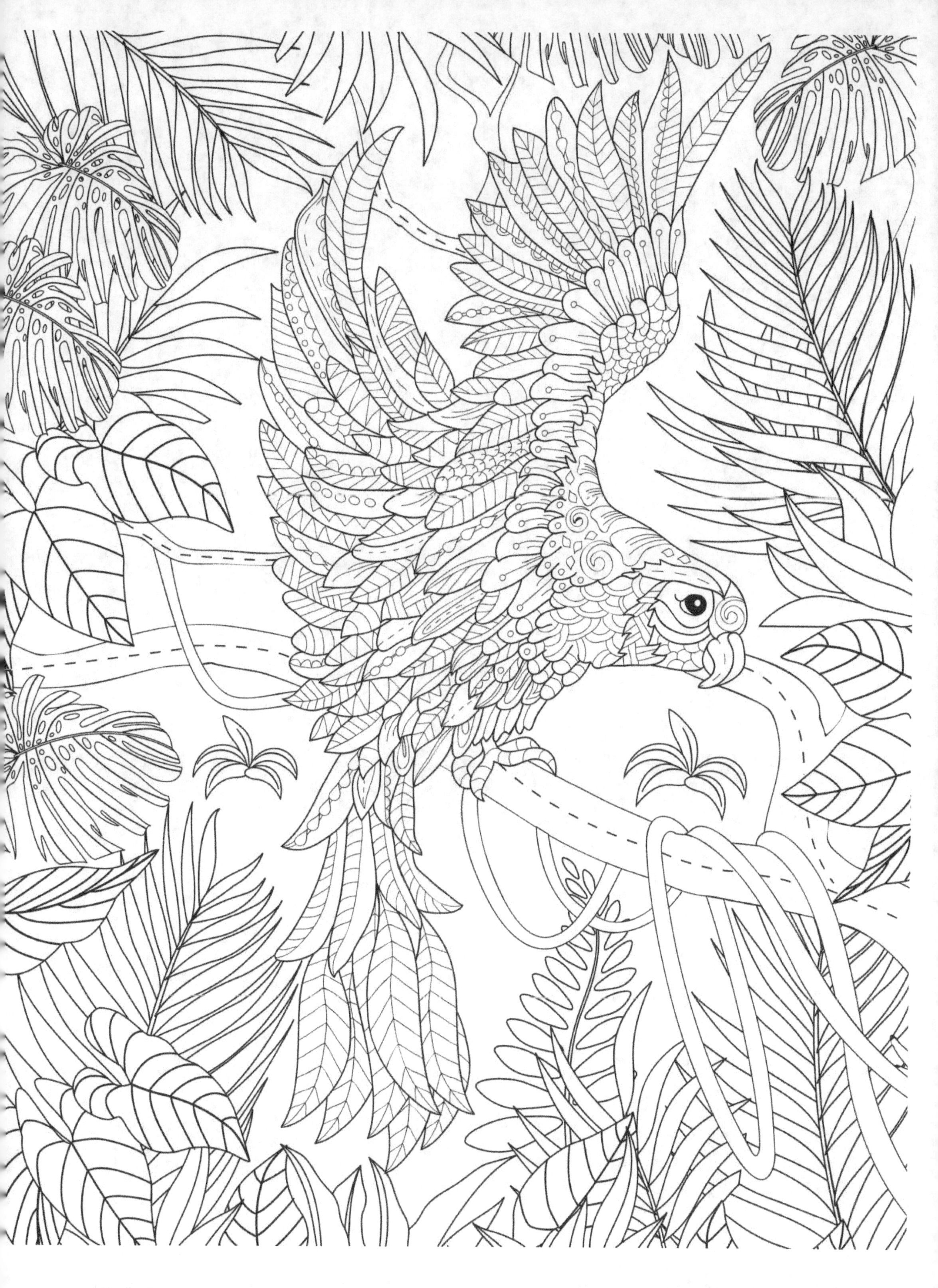

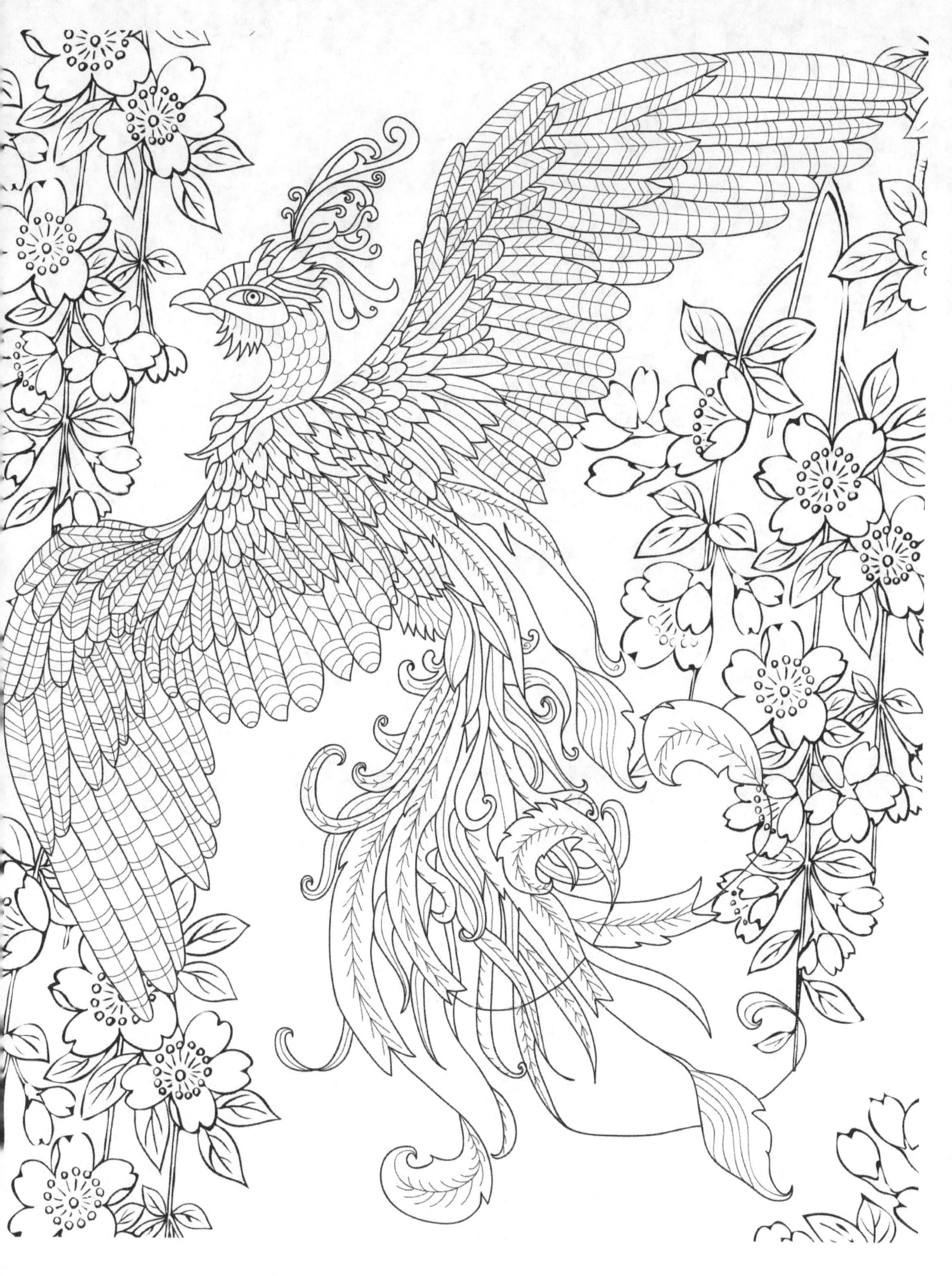

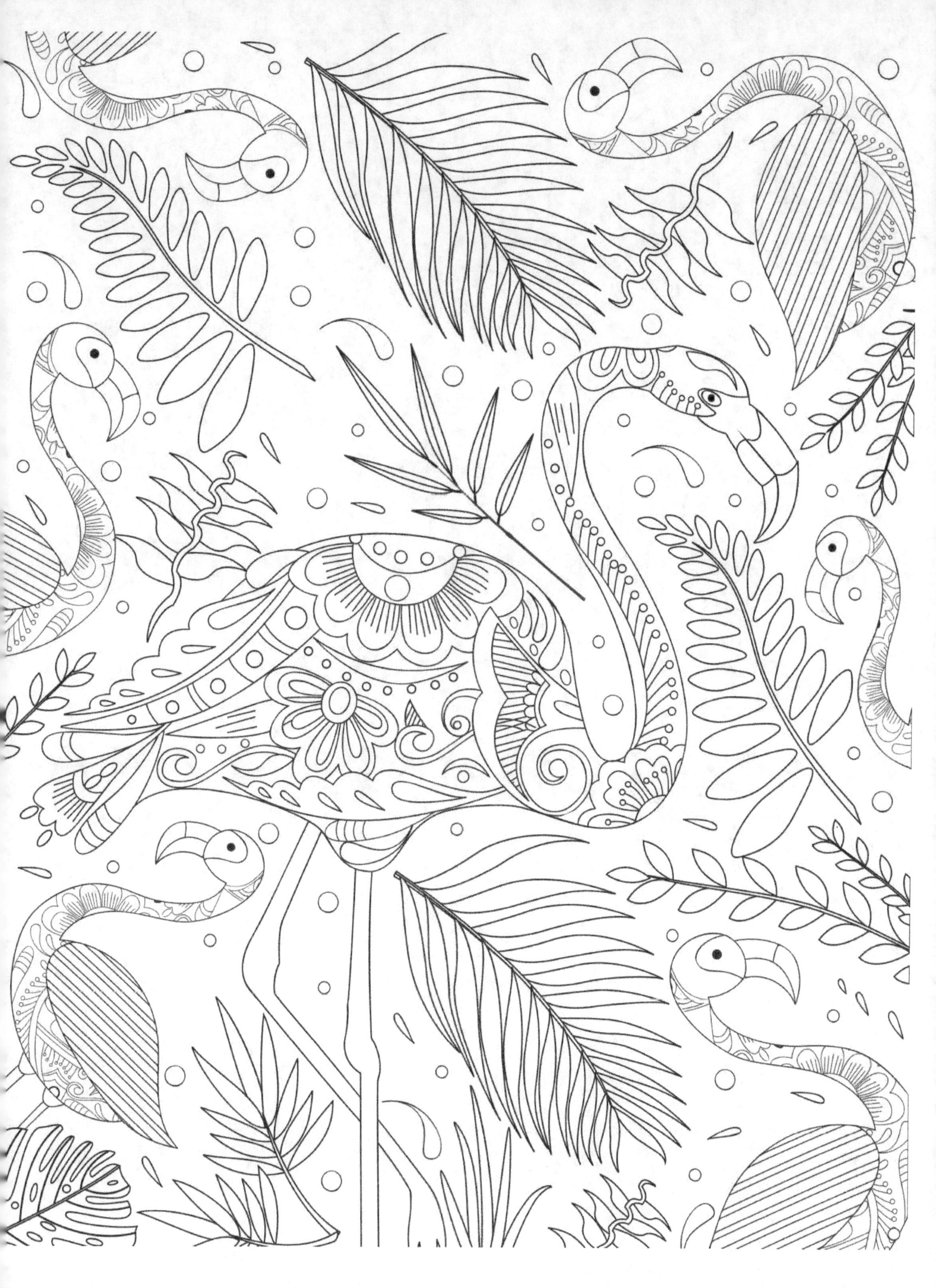

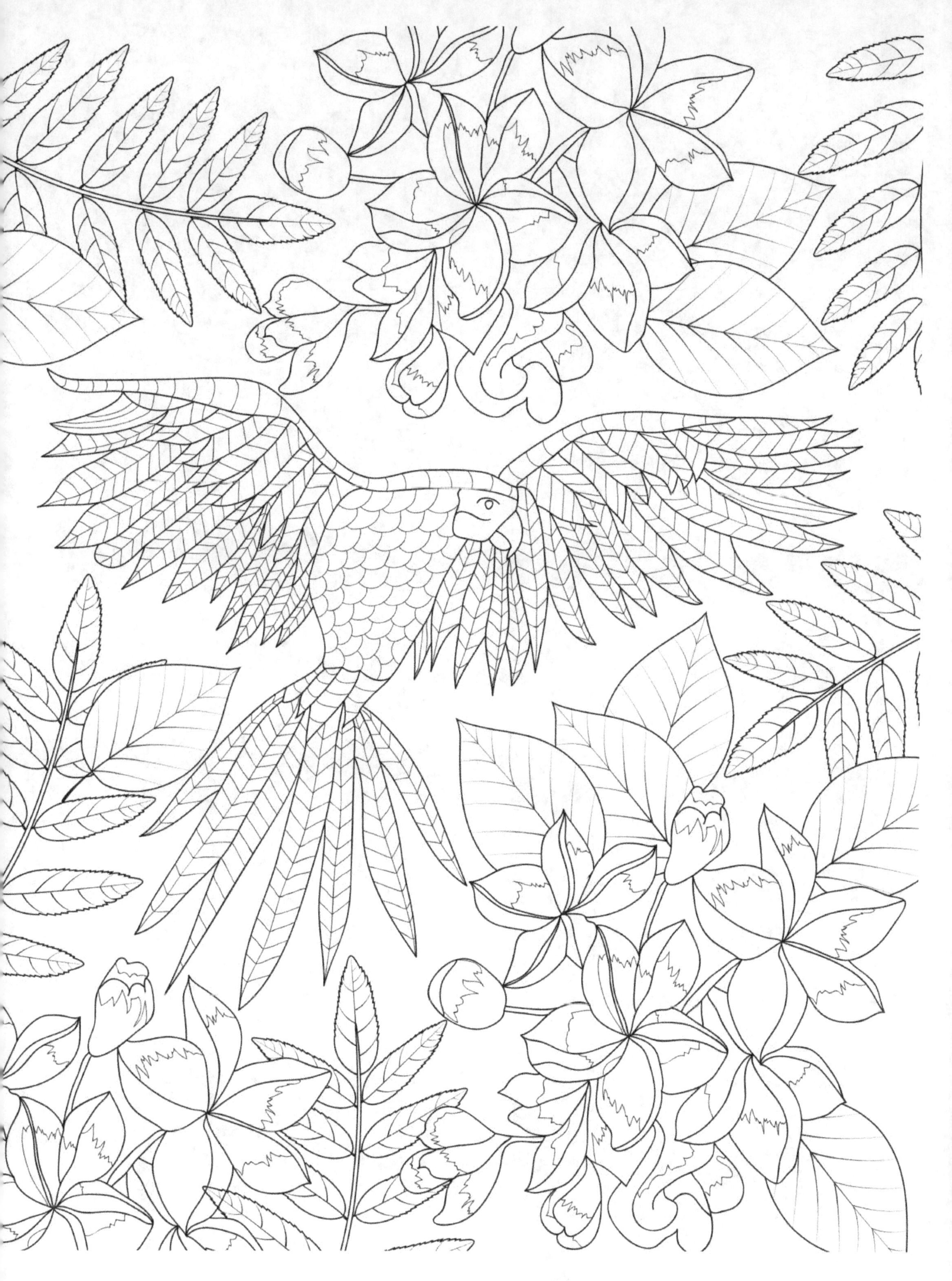

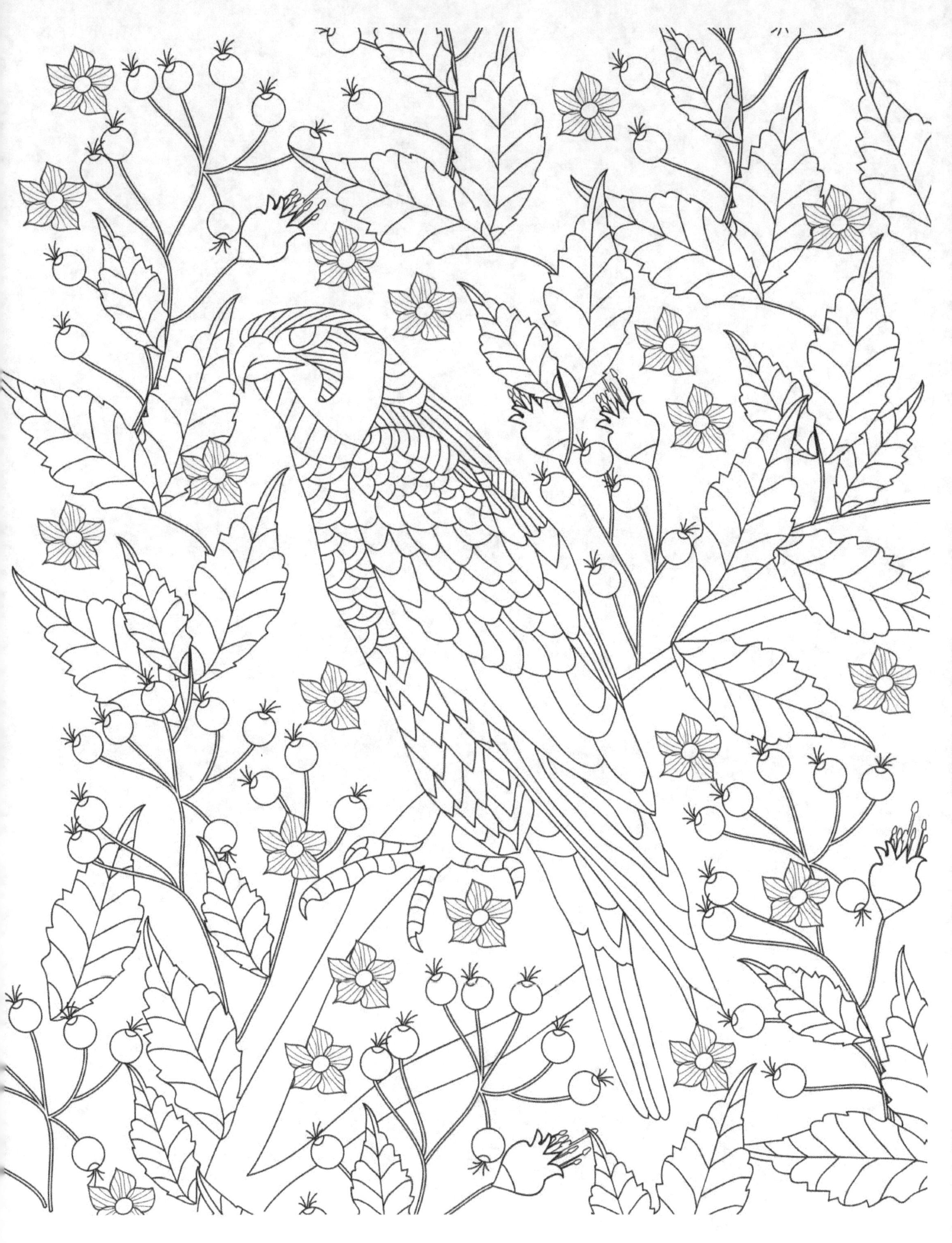

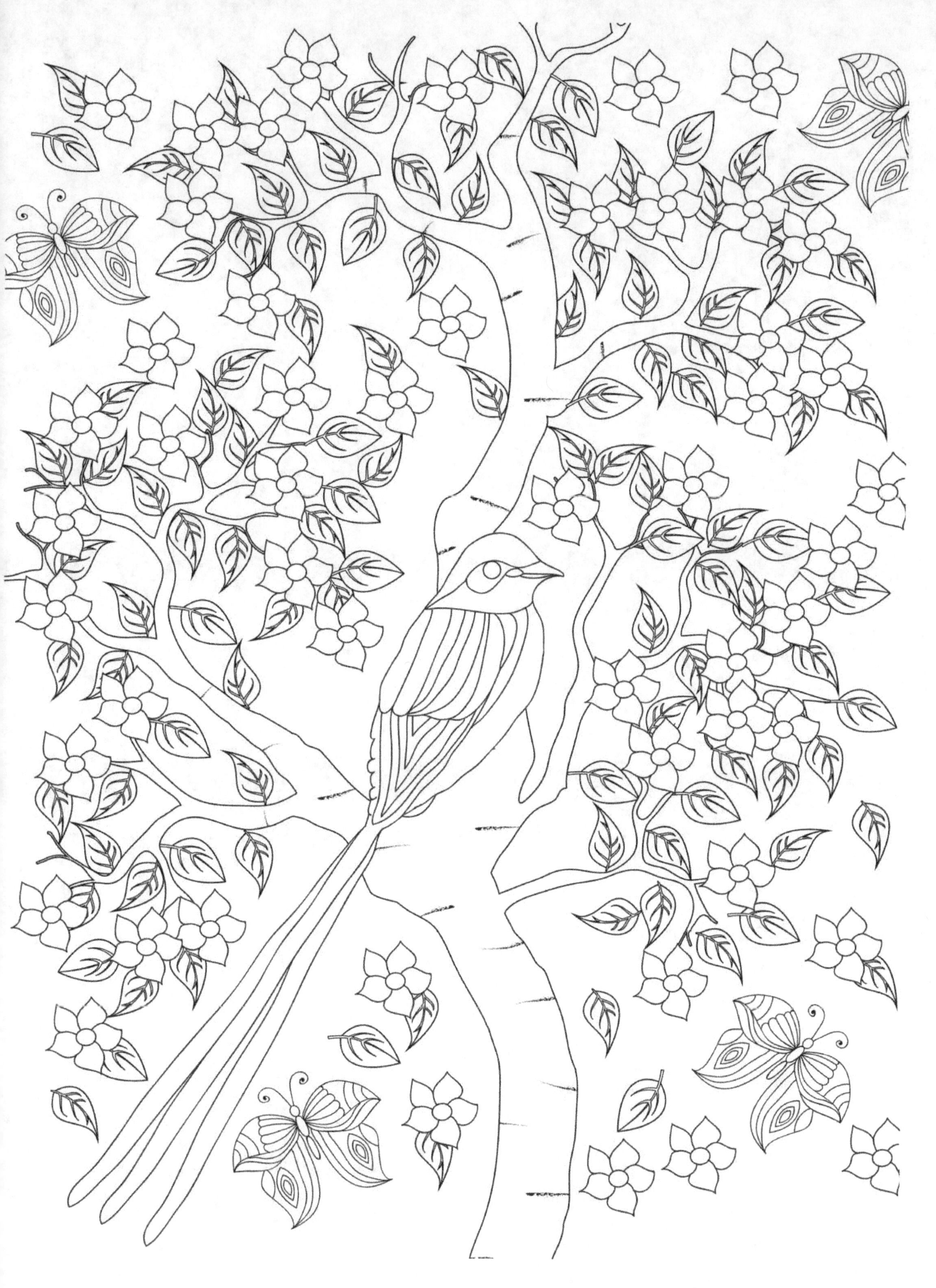

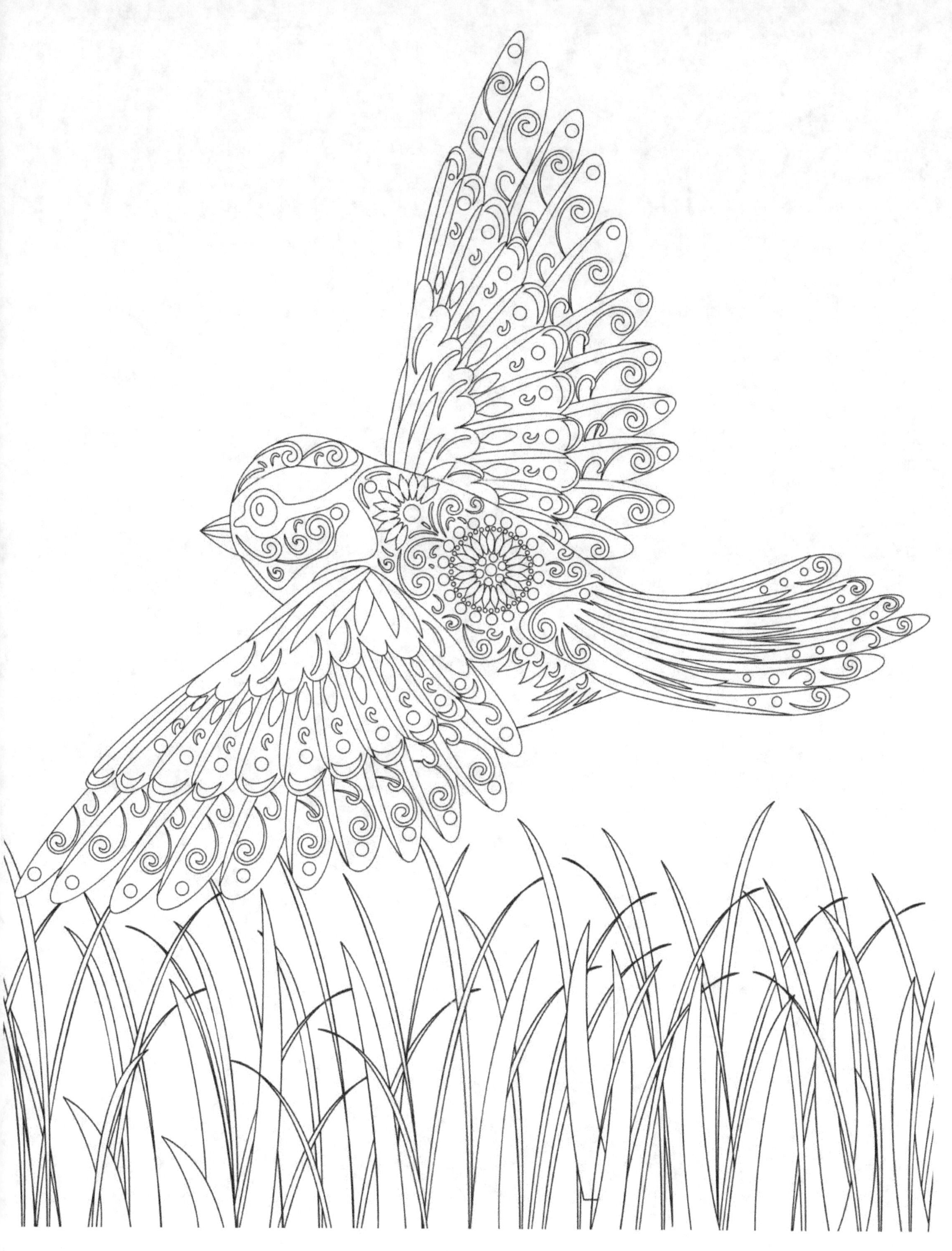

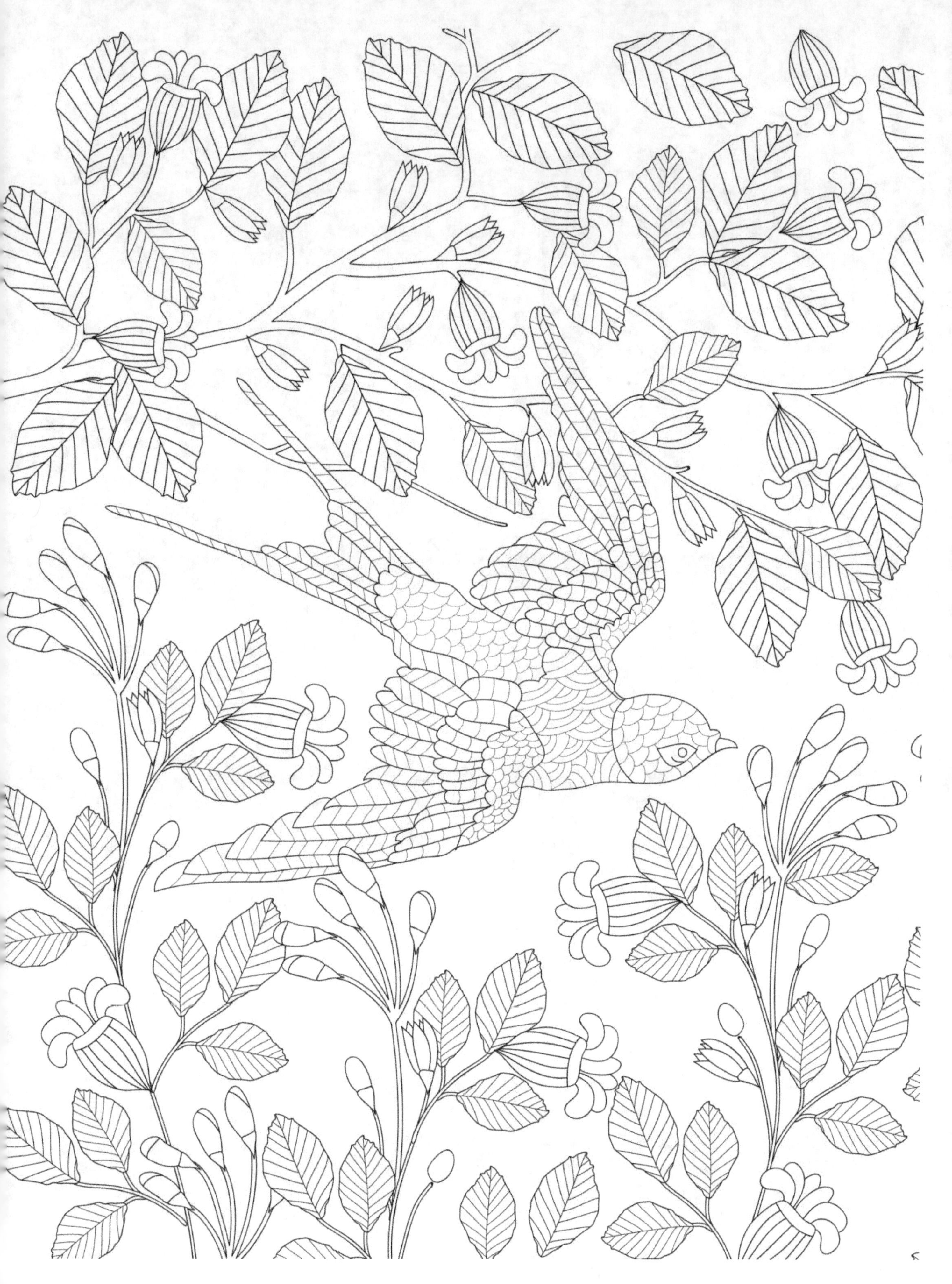

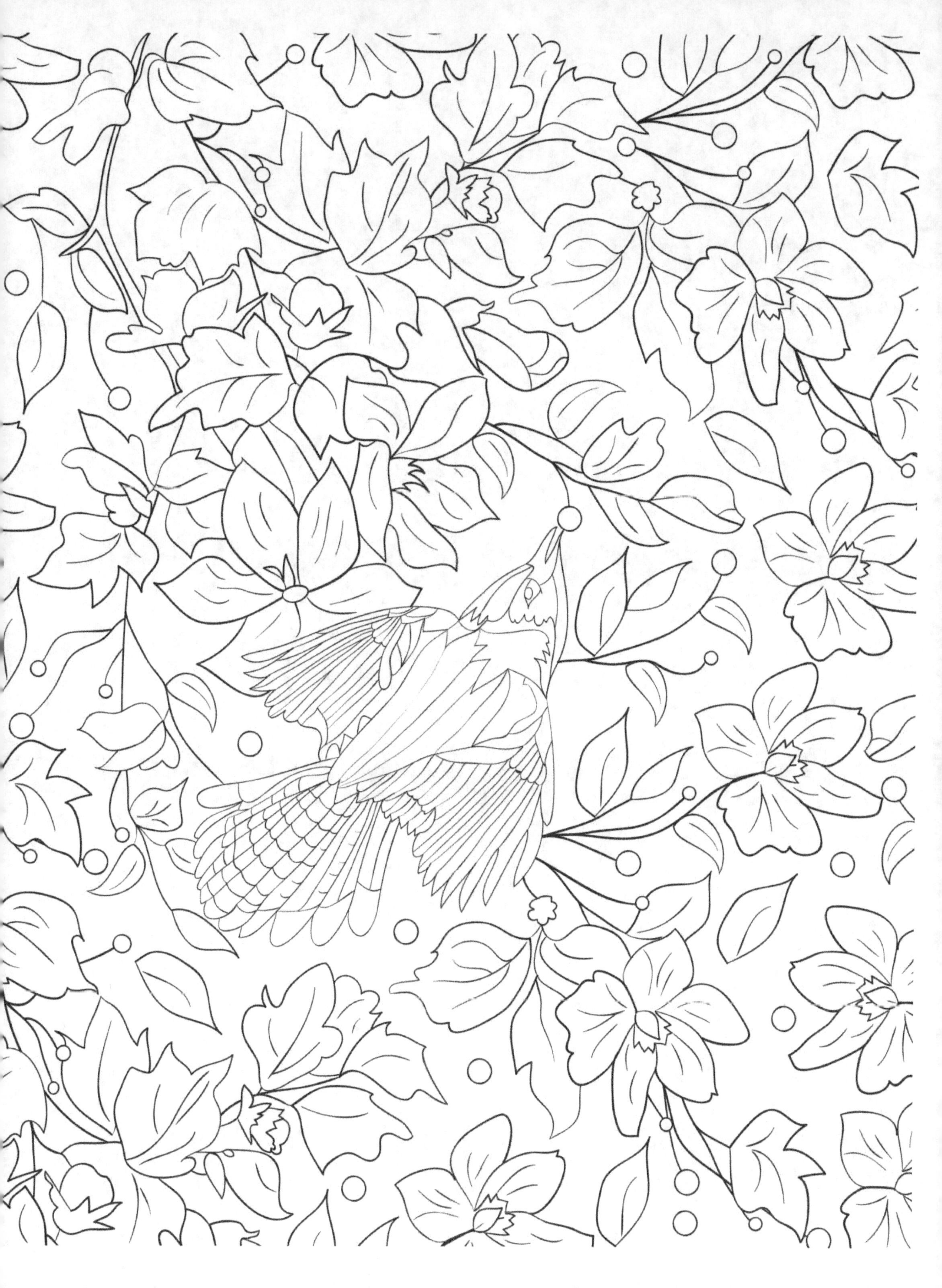

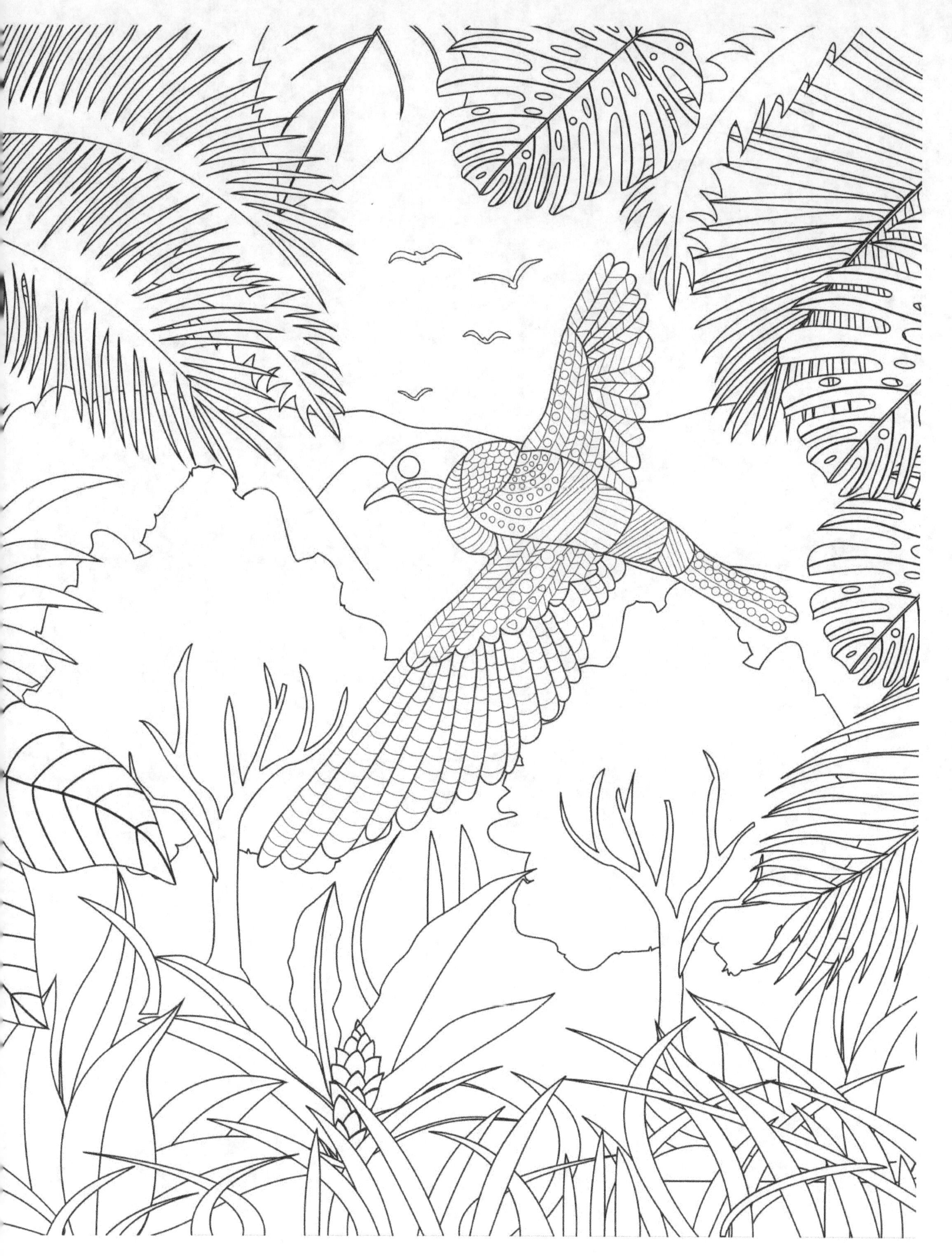

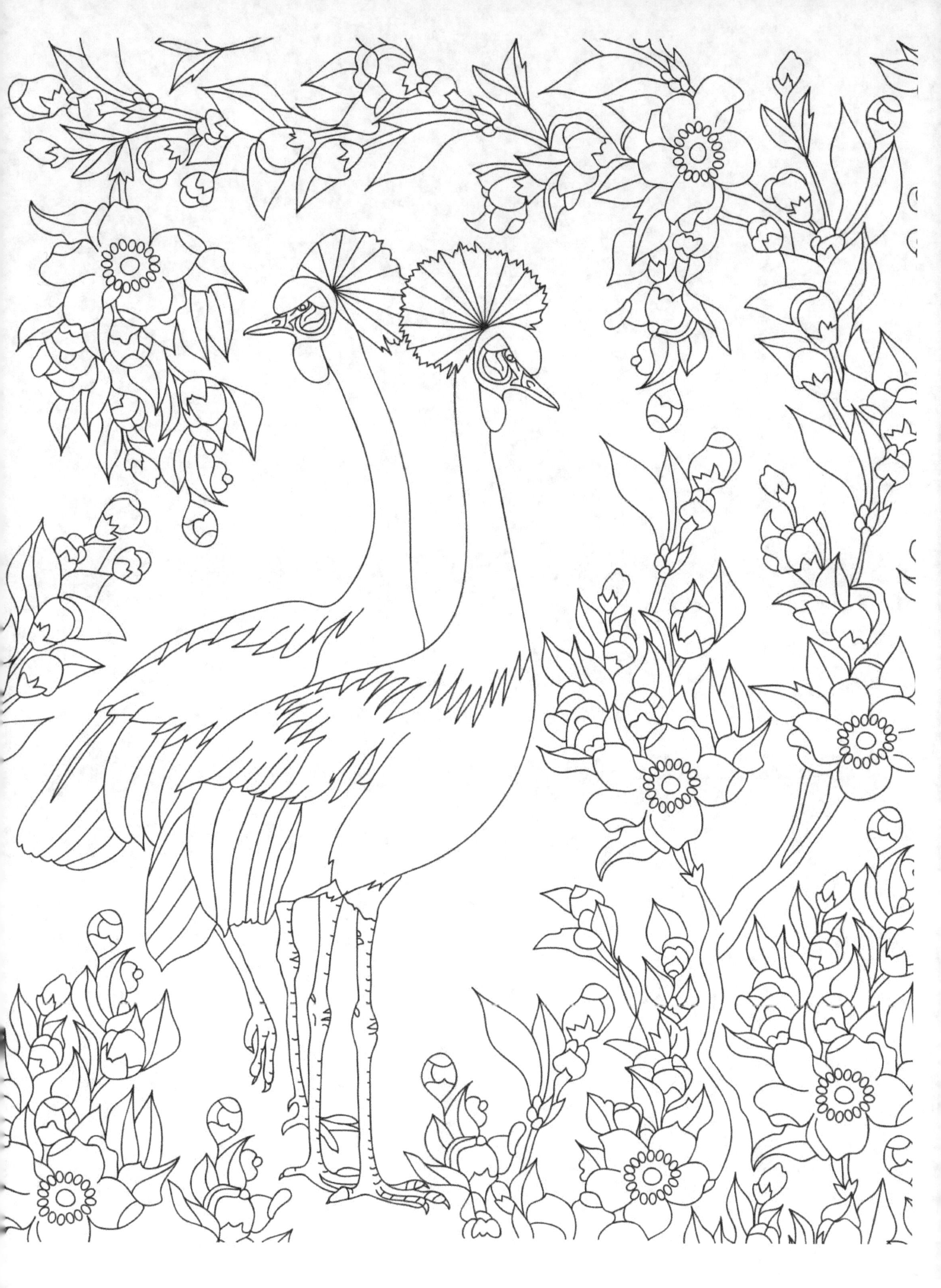

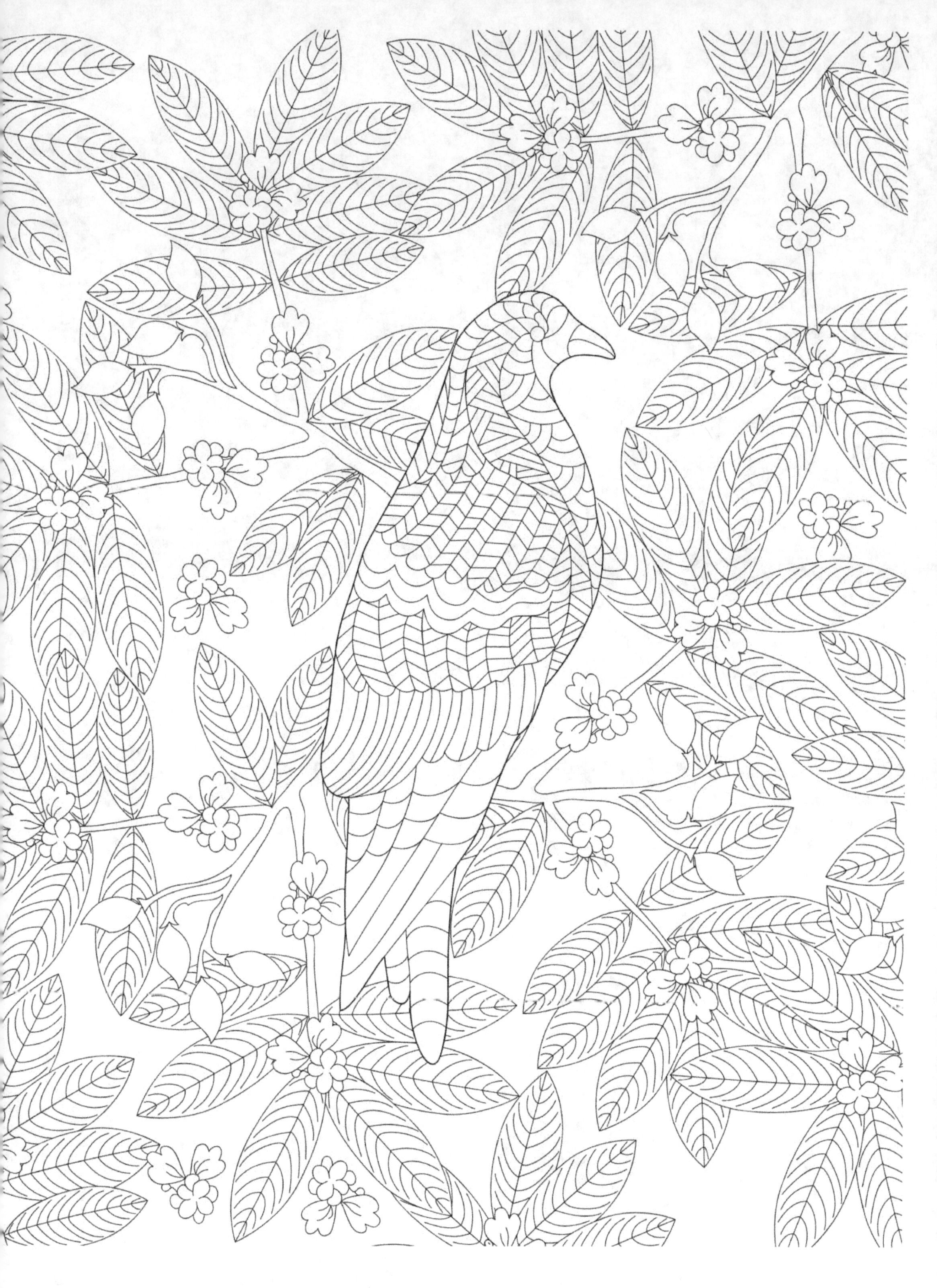

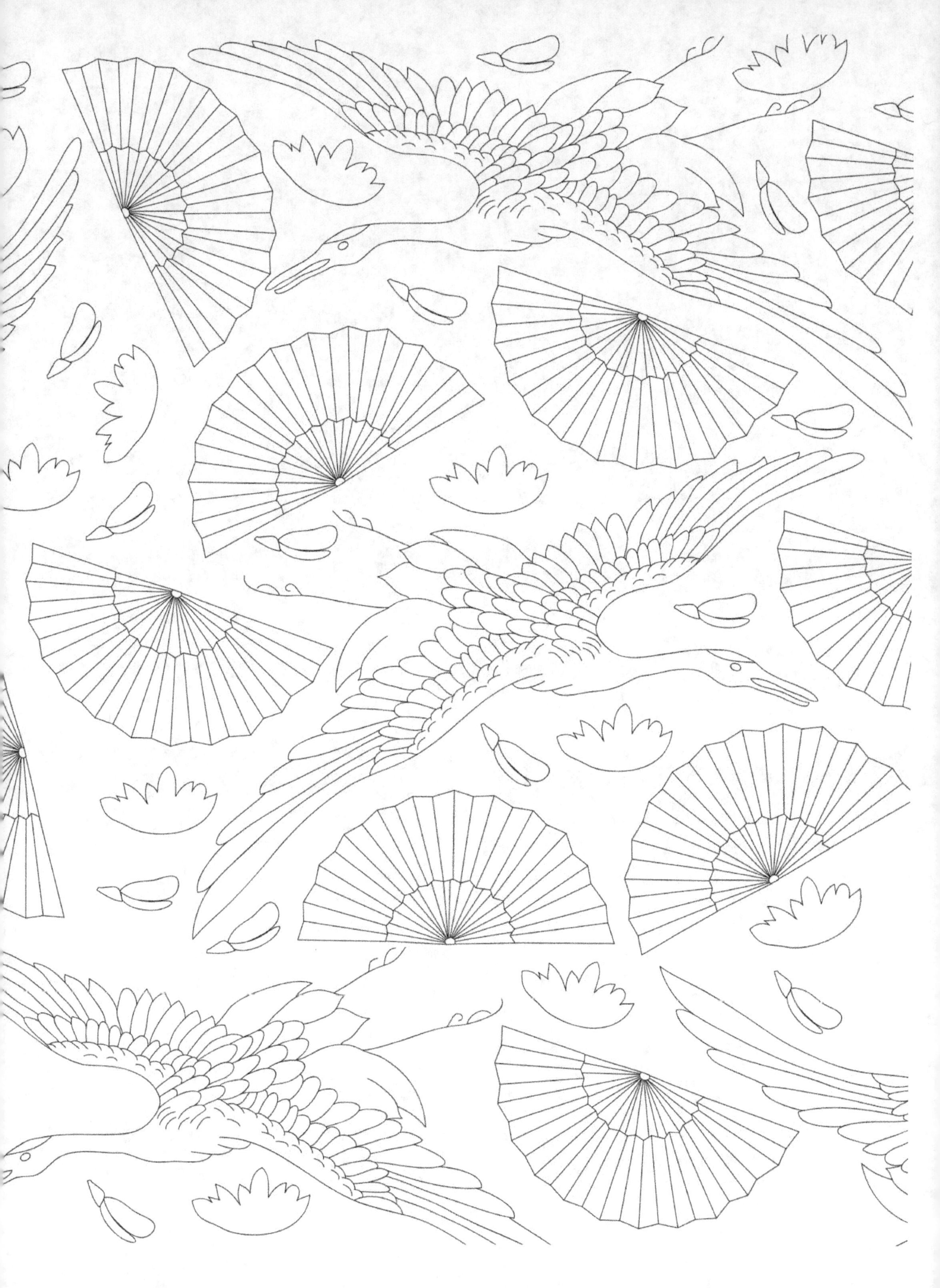

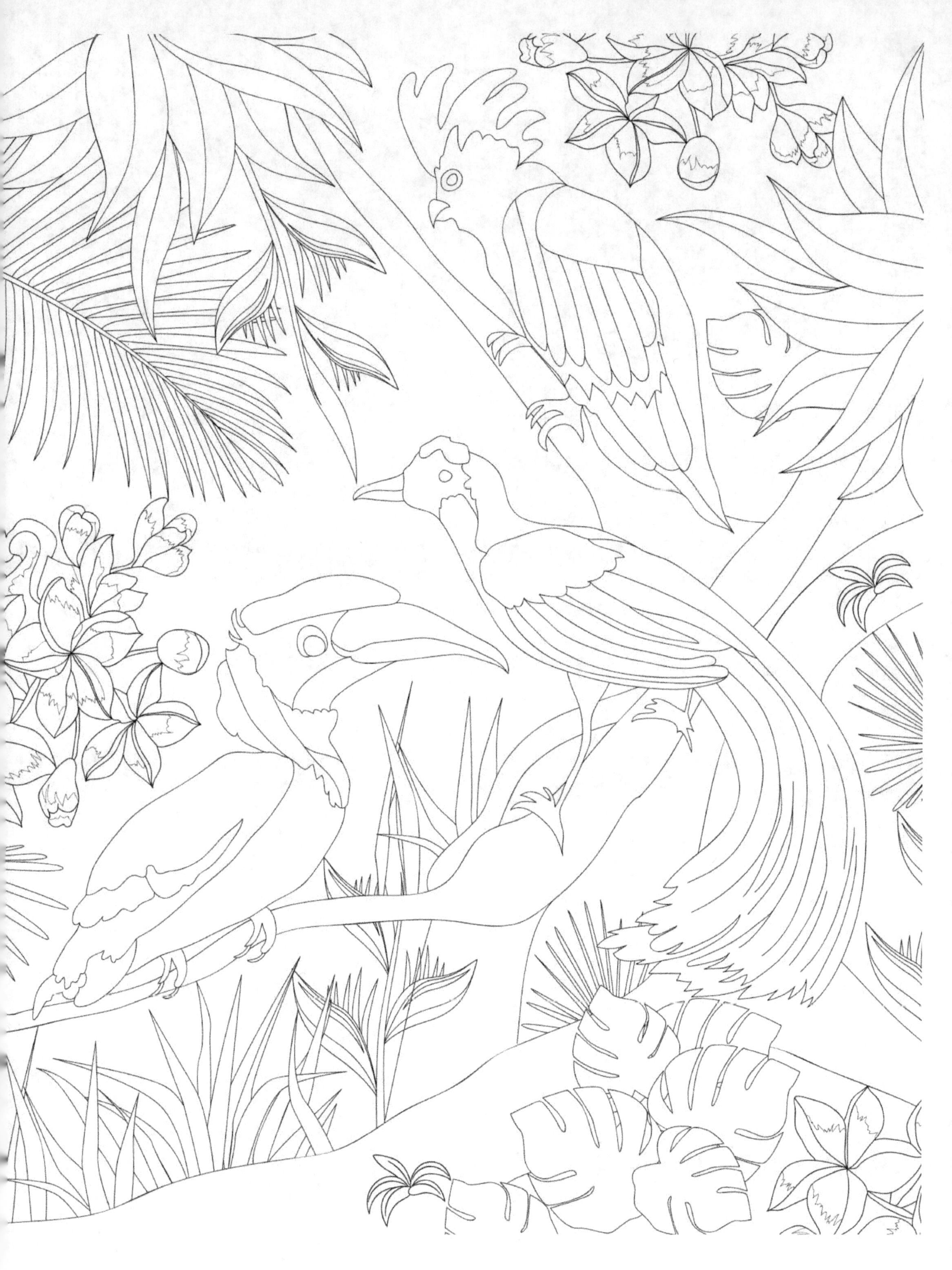

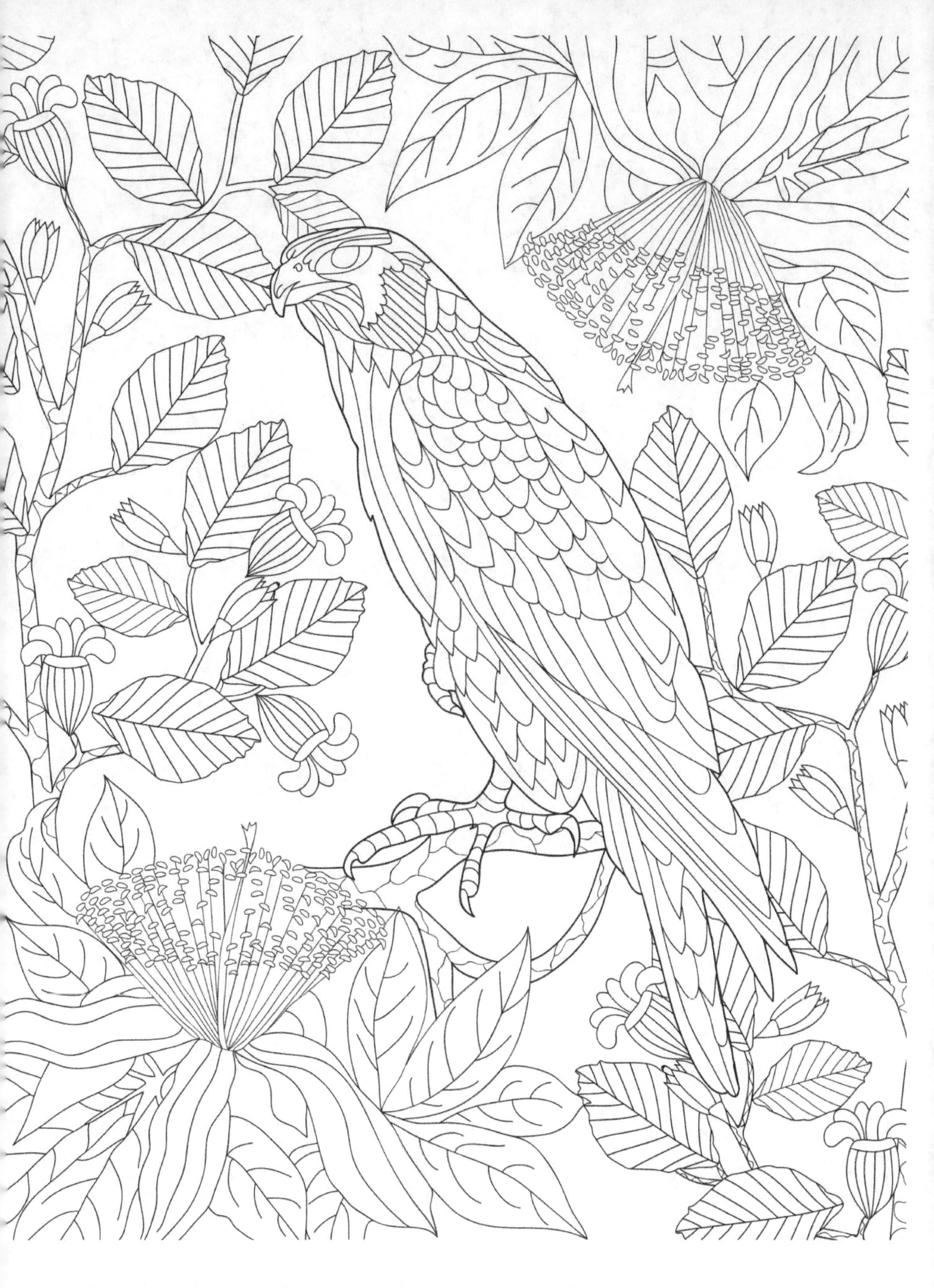

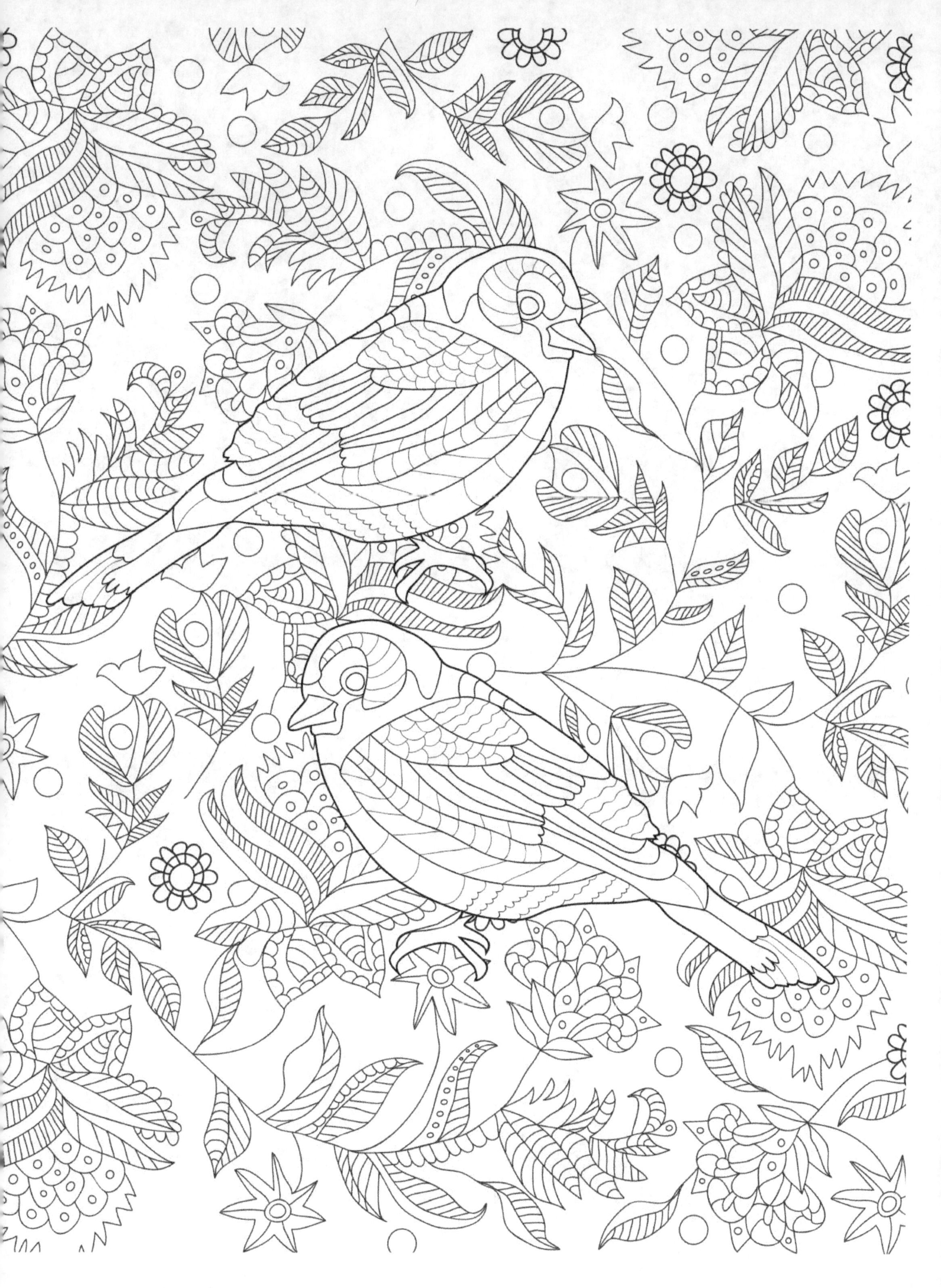

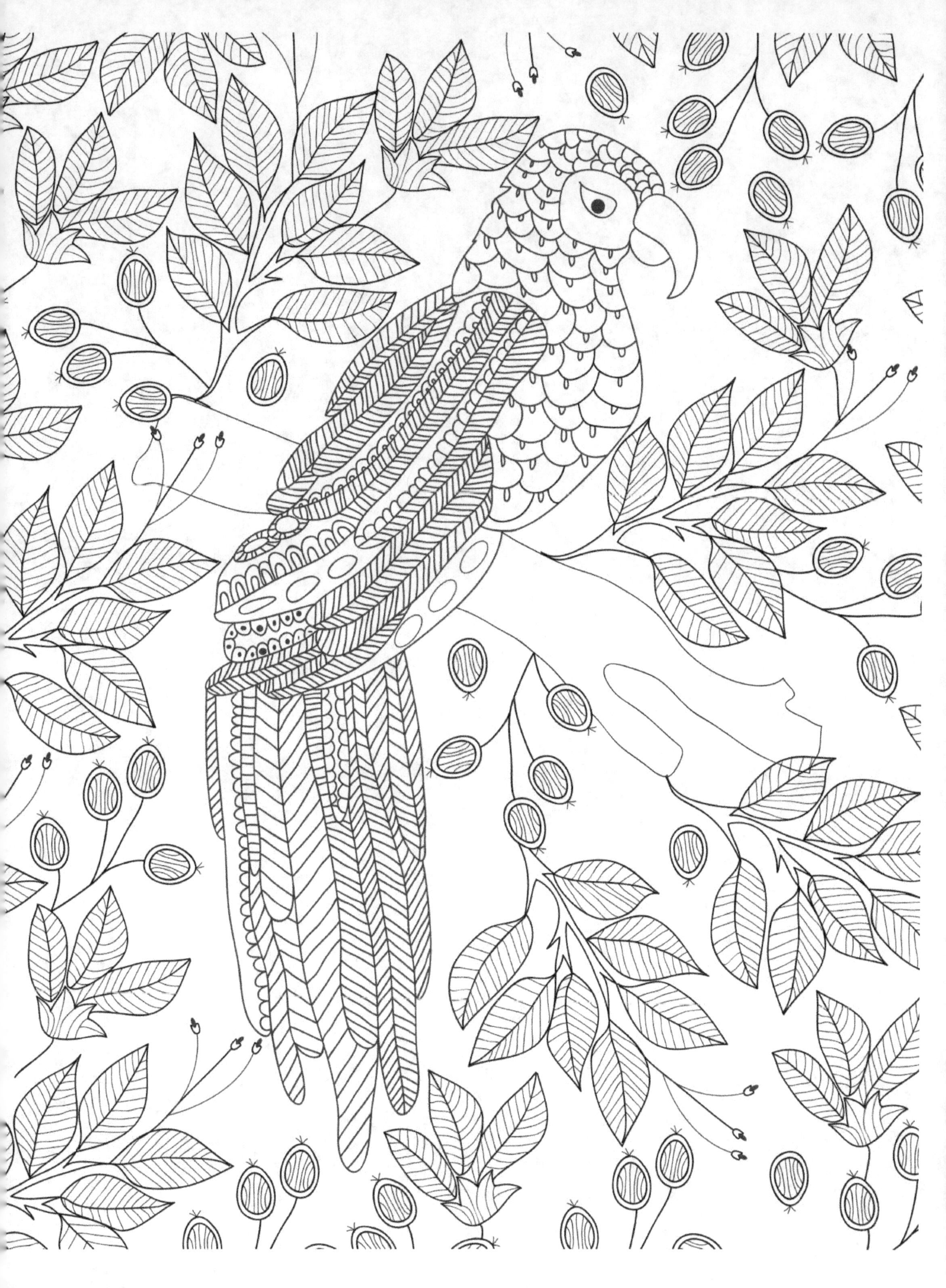

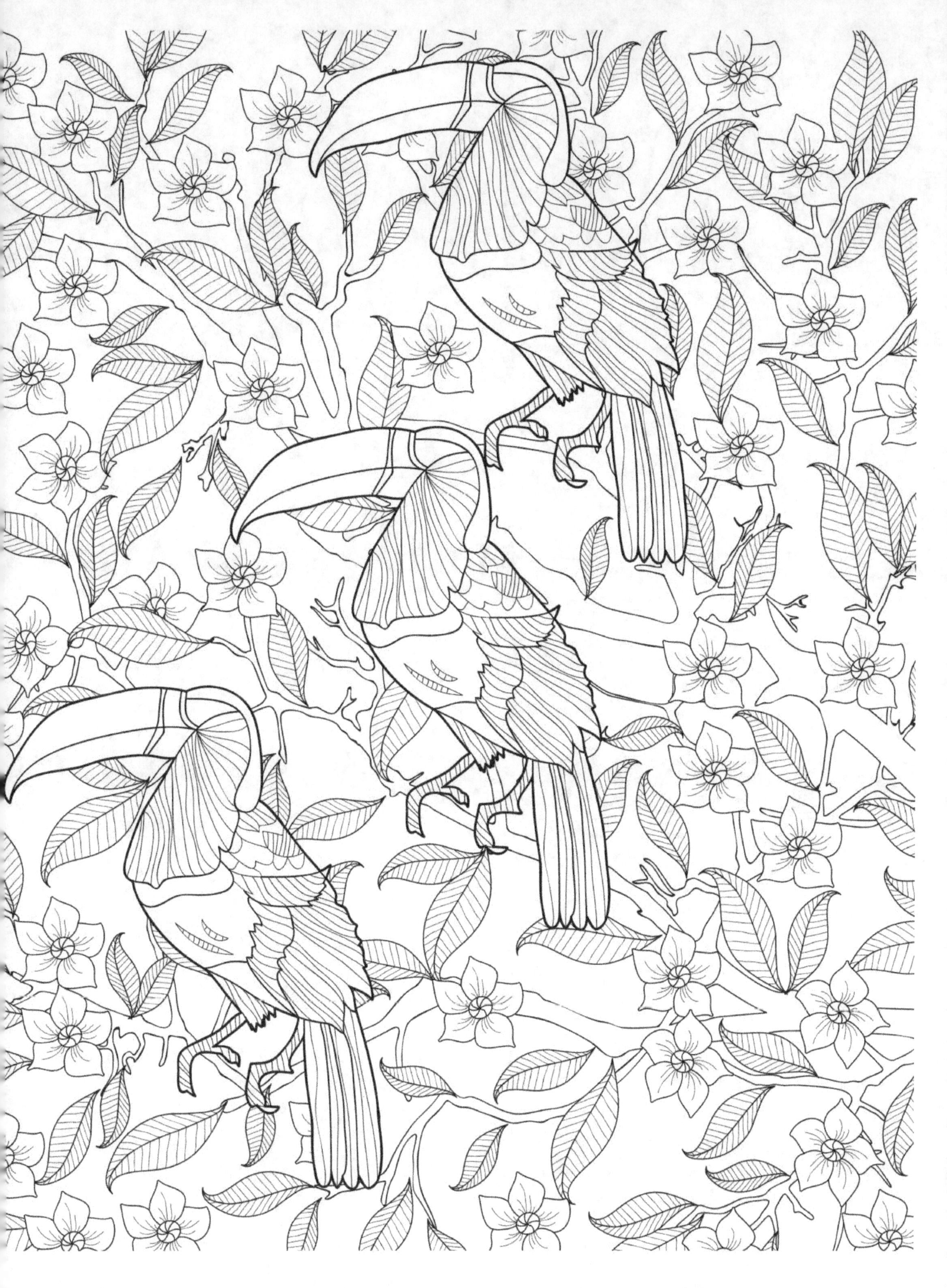

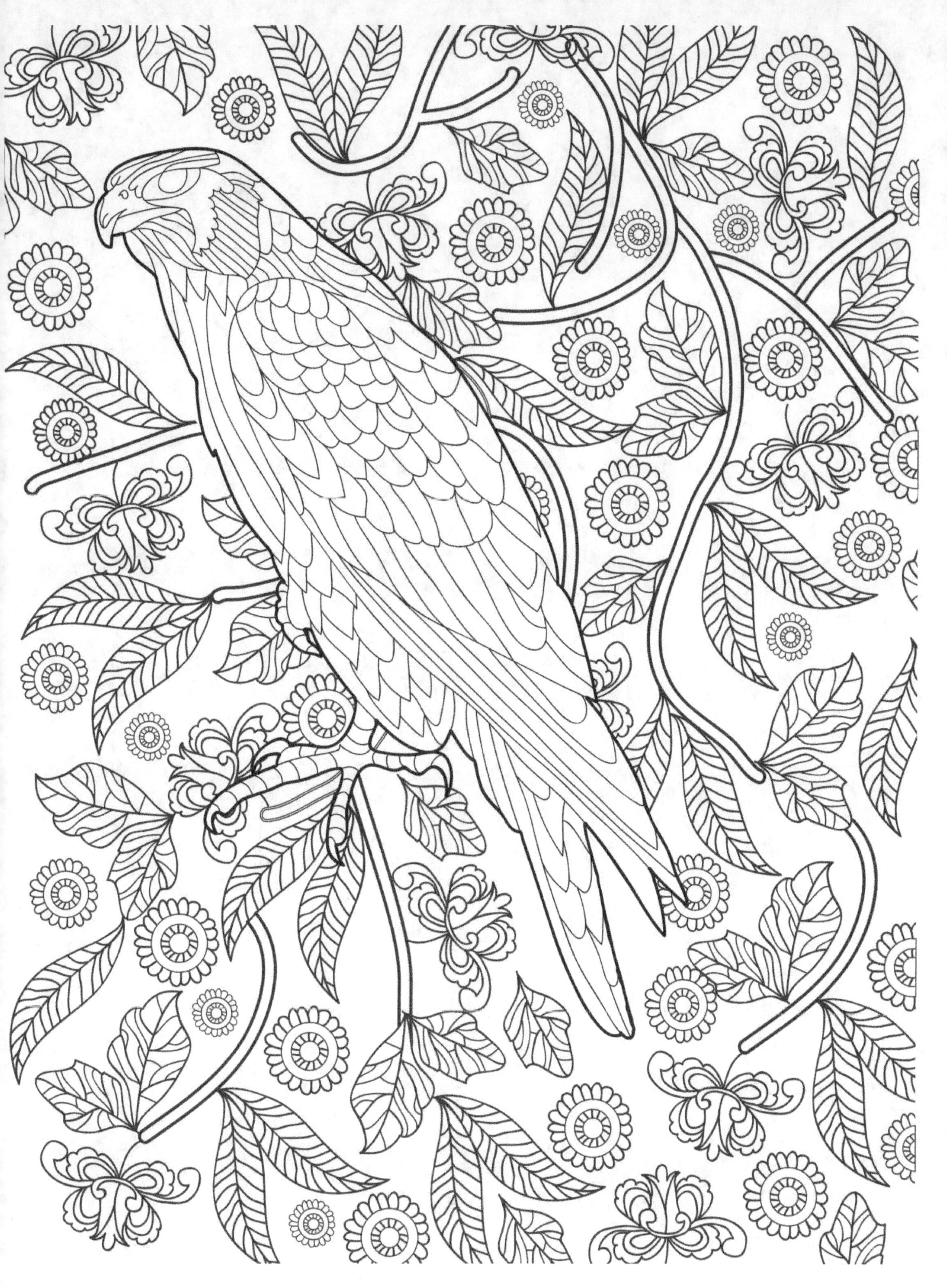